A *Home Start* In
READING

Ruth Beechick

arrow press

Pollock Pines, California

Other books in this series for grades K to 3 include:

An Easy Start in Arithmetic
A Strong Start in Language

For grades 4 to 8:

You CAN Teach Your Child Successfully

Printed in the United States of America
Distributed by Education Services, 6410 Raleigh, Arvada CO 80003

Contents

Introduction

Congratulations on your decision to teach your child at home. Home is the best of all possible environments for learning. These five steps to reading are for you if you intend to be your child's main teacher or if you wish to supplement the teaching he or she gets at school.

As you read this parent guide, you will find that the simple steps to reading remove the mystique that too often surrounds the subject. There is no real mystery about reading; it is only common sense for people like you, who read regularly and who buy books on how to teach their children. Learn the five steps, know where you are headed, and confidence will be yours.

This is one of the easiest guides to reading instruction that you will ever find. Extraneous theories and arguments about reading have been left out. Impractical, ivory-tower ideas are not here either. What you will find is a straight path through the reading maze, a path that has been traveled by hundreds of children which the author has led to a life of reading.

When can you start? Probably as soon as you familiarize yourself with the five steps. If your child is very young—say, anywhere from birth to four years old—you can start with Step 1 and move in the next few years through the rest of the steps. If your child is kindergarten or primary age you may plunge in at any step that seems to fit the child's needs. And if your child is older yet, but does not have a good start in reading, dip into these steps at various points. Give him anything he has missed or hasn't yet mastered.

How long can you use this guide? In grade level terms, the guide takes you through early reading, up to about fourth grade, the level where children can use their reading skills to learn history or science or any other subject found in books. In terms of age, the time varies widely. More on this in the steps themselves.

What curriculum or books do you need? This homespun, natural system of reading does not require expensive teaching materials. Actually, all you need are this guide and easy books that are available around your home and local libraries. A good argument for using homemade flashcards is that you won't be using them long, anyway.

When you individualize for your child, you (or the child) make flashcards for something he needs to learn. Hopefully, in a few days, or at most a few weeks, he learns them and you move on to new lessons. You don't feel obliged to do more in order to "get your money's worth" out of a set of commercial cards. The same can be said for workbooks. Once the money is spent, there is a temptation to make the child work every line of every page whether he needs it or not. Parents then find themselves teaching a book or a course instead of teaching the child. But such materials are not precluded when you use this guide. You and your child may enjoy using them and may want them at various times, and you will find that practically any such materials easily fit into the steps described herein.

This guide is arranged with the five steps of reading described in the next five sections. In each section you get an explanation and overview of the step itself. In steps 2 through 5 you get basic teaching methods and a list of games and activities for adding occasional variety to the basics. In the latter steps you also get guidelines for teaching writing and spelling, as these skills must grow along with reading.

Before embarking on the steps, we pause for a word of caution. When any learning or developmental process is laid out in steps, the typical American reaction is to try to move children through the steps earlier and faster. Our ambitious, achievement-oriented culture seems to demand this. If you have that common American characteristic, this caution is not to say you should change your values and desire less than the best for your child. But it is to remind you that there are other considerations besides moving up the steps. For one, there is the principle of optimum timing which will be explained later. For another, there is quality. The steps undergird a lifetime of reading and learning. So build the foundation by thoroughness and mastery, not just speed. And a third consideration is enjoyment. Too much pressure on a child can cause a dislike of reading and of books. The very goal you want the most can be lost. So move ahead at your child's own timing.

And now, on with the five steps for teaching your child to read.

STEP 1: Prereading

This step begins in babyhood with all the things you've heard about loving the child and letting him grow up confident and with a good measure of self-esteem. But let's assume that most of you reading this guide have already passed that time in your child's life.

If you are reading this guide, you probably are wondering when and how to begin teaching "reading." First, let's take up the question of when. That's very important. There has been much talk about it in recent years, and no doubt you can find among your friends both "early starters" and "late starters." The early starters have read books about how to teach their baby to read. They have labels on furniture, appliances, and doors all over the house. Their baby plays with word cards every day. The late starters are more relaxed. They read books too—the "late is better" variety. They read to their children. They teach them to cook and garden and help fix the car. And they won't be upset if a child doesn't show a desire to read until age eight or so.

Which of your friends are right? This guide will generally take you somewhere between those two extremes as it helps you individualize for your own child. In walking between the extremes, we probably lean more toward "late" than "early," not because there is anything especially wrong with the early systems, but because we have seen more damage done to the early children. It usually is not the baby who shows any readiness or eagerness to learn to read early, but it is too often an over-anxious mother pushing for it.

Occasionally in a family, older children will play school with a younger sibling and teach the child to read. In one family, the children sprawled around a newspaper each night and taught the youngest the letters and sounds in headlines. It was similar to playing with a doll, only this one was live, and particularly bright. She learned to read before age three and came to no harm because of it. Some mothers may enjoy playing with their "dolls" in this way and the children will not be harmed. Unfortunately, other mothers are feeding their own egos when they do this. Wanting their children to outdo other children, they pressure, and damage both the child's personality and the relationship between child and mother.

It is true that some children can learn to read remarkably early. But the fact that they *can* does not necessarily mean they *should. Should* is another question. One school district set up an experiment to help decide this question. Some kindergartners in the district received extensive instruction in reading. Others spent the same amount of time learning science. They melted ice. They observed thermometers in hot and cold places. They played with magnets, grew plants, learned about animal life, and so on. Books and pictures were available for these children if they wanted them, but no formal lessons in reading were held.

And what did the school district learn? By third grade the "science" children were far ahead of the "reading" children in their reading scores. The reason? Their vocabularies and thinking skills were more advanced. They could read on more topics and understand higher level materials. The "reading" children, by starting earlier, used up a lot of learning time on the skills of reading, while the "science" children spent the time learning real stuff. And when they did begin reading, they were older and knew more and learned in a fraction of the time that the others took.

This research and others like it are compelling. They drive home the fact that each child has only a limited amount of time in his early years. That time can be squandered in trying to teach reading before the "optimum" time for it. Or it can be used wisely in teaching "real stuff" that the child is ready for. If you are the teacher, the choice is yours.

The real stuff your child learns does not have to be only science. Science is a natural because children are curious about the world around them, and you can capitalize on that curiosity. But you can teach also about music, art, literature, money, work, safety, God, people, and everything else you and your child are interested in.

All such teaching is "prereading" instruction. It is getting ready for reading. Everything your child learns increases his vocabulary and develops his thinking skills. Now, you have been doing this for your child all along. How did he learn words so far? How did he learn the grammar necessary to form sentences? How did he learn to tell the chocolate milk carton from the white milk carton? The science research described above seems to be telling you to keep up that kind of informal teaching a little longer than most people would advise you to. The American attitude that "earlier is better" will die hard, in spite of research evidence to the contrary.

Prereading instruction, then, is wider than the whole world. Teach about the cooking and cleaning going on in your kitchen. Teach good eating habits, nutrition, care of teeth. And teach about the stars and the God who made them. Solve problems. How can we arrange the sleeping when Grandma comes to visit? How can we keep baby brother from eating the crayons? Read aloud to your child. Teach nursery rhymes. Ask questions and let the child ask you questions.

Some readers will say, "I've done all that. Now when do I start actual reading instruction?"

If you are in tune with your child, it is quite easy to tell when. Children have different ways of letting you know. Some begin asking about words and letters. Some learn favorite books by heart and sit reading them.

Put out trial balloons. Teach the child to write or pronounce one or more sounds. Is he interested in learning them? Or does he resist?

Your observations of the child and your trial balloons will tell you when to start. And the same skills will tell you all along the path just how fast to move.

Read the next step carefully. It likely is different from first reading steps that you have heard of elsewhere.

STEP 2: Beginning

Did you ever stop to think that you don't need to know the names of letters in order to read? That's right. To read *cat* or *dog*, you must know the sound of each letter but you do not need to know its name.

With a grasp of that principle, you have a shortcut to your child's reading. Do not burden her at the beginning with learning the names of twenty-six letters. Start by teaching the forms of the letters and their sounds. Begin with the child's own name and other high interest words. Later, for thoroughness, you can use a set of cards or a chart or list.

Let's say, for instance, that your child's name is Jenny. Print it with the *J* capitalized and the other letters in lower case. Say, "This says 'Jenny.' " Let the child look, trace with her fingers or a crayon, or make a copy, according to her ability. If this is the first time, you may guide her finger to trace the *J* only.

Take a shortcut with writing, too. Don't burden the child at the beginning with lines. Don't force her to decide how high to make each letter, how to make it sit on a line, when to go below the line, and so forth. Let her concentrate only on the form of the letter. Use unlined paper. Lines can come later when she has control of the forms.

Back to the word *Jenny:* trace the *J*, make the sound /j/, and say "Jenny." (In this guide sounds are given between slashes and letters are given in italics.) After she recognizes her name and can print it, you can branch outward from that knowledge. Print *Jelly.* "J-jelly." Print *Jet.* "J-jet." Then print jelly and jet with lower case j's. Move on to jam, jump, and other words. She can print a *j* and you can finish the word that you or she thinks of. Build her awareness of other sounds besides the *j* in these words.

All this is done without ever using the name "jay" for the letter. You can play with words in this manner for quite some time in the life of your child, not always with her name, but sometimes with words from a book such as *The Cat in the Hat,* or with any word that catches her fancy.

That is Step 2 in teaching reading: teach the forms and sounds of a few letters. Notice that you have bypassed learning the alphabet and learning the letter names. You have moved directly to the skill needed in sounding out words. It won't hurt Jenny if she learns the alphabet and letter names from watching television or from other children. She eventually will need to know them. But now in the beginning, you can strip reading down to its essentials. This makes it an exciting mental challenge—a matter of understanding and not just a matter of memorizing a lot of phonics facts that Jenny is not ready to use yet.

With one or two vowels and with a few consonants now in your pupil's head, she is ready for the next step, which is the most crucial point in her reading career. Be sure you understand the concept in Step 3 so you will recognize when your child has attained it.

Activities for Step 2

1. Ask the child to look around the room and see what else she can find that begins like *pan.* (Paper, pencil, popcorn, etc.) Look out the window and see what she can find that begins like s-s-sidewalk.

2. For an active child, let her jump up two stairsteps when she names a word in the game above. She jumps two more steps when she names another. How high can she get?

3. Print sounds onto cards. Place three or four cards in a row and say each sound, having your child say them after you. Then say, "Listen to me now and stop me when I make a mistake." When the child "catches" you in a mistake, start at the beginning again and make a mistake in a different place. At first you may make absurd mistakes, such as a motorcycle sound or a dog's bark. Later, make the wrong letter sound. Mix the cards and repeat.

4. Hide a sound (letter) card behind a blank card. Slowly pull it upward and see how soon your child can tell which sound is coming up the elevator.

5. Place each sound you are teaching on a page of a scrapbook. Have the child look for pictures which begin with that sound.

6. Place a "sound for the day" or "sound for the week" on your child's bulletin board or on the refrigerator. During the day add words or pictures that match. Add fun by starting with a picture or real object such as a stuffed animal. Call it kangaroo day when you work on /k/ sound and panda day when you work on /p/ sound.

7. Have the child make placecards for the family dinner table. She may print only the first sound or, if she can, the full names.

STEP 3: Blending

During Step 2 you did not teach all the letters or all their sounds. That's the dull, memorizing, way of teaching. Your goal, instead, was to start your child toward the exciting discovery that the sounds blend together to make words. That discovery, itself, is Step 3.

When your child knows a few consonants and one or two vowels quite well, you can begin working on Step 3—blending. Let's say, for instance, that he has learned the short sound of a, which we will write here as /ă/. That is the sound of a as in dad.

Many people teach only the short sound of a vowel at first. And later when the child can blend well, they introduce additional sounds. This makes sense for two reasons. The first reason is that it minimizes the child's memory task. With only a few letters and sounds he can actually "read" by blending sounds together into words. And he is not confused with a lot of other sounds in his memory that he is not using yet. It's another shortcut; it gets you directly to the heart of the task.

A second reason for teaching the short sound first, is that it is used more often. For instance, when a is found in words, 70% of the time it sounds like /ă/, 25% of the time it sounds like /ay/, and about 5% of the time it sounds like /ah/. There are a few other sounds for a, but these three are the major ones, and all that a beginner needs to learn.

So now, let's suppose that your Johnny knows short o and short a sounds. And he knows a few consonant sounds: /n/ because it is in his name, and /p/ and /t/ because you made a point to teach them. To start this blending lesson, use only one vowel and print it on a chalkboard or paper above the consonants thus:

a

n p t

Point to the a and say /ă/ (the short sound as in dad). Teach Johnny to say /ă/ each time you point to it. Then slide your finger or pointer from a to n, and say the word an. Have Johnny say the word each time you point to those two sounds. Teach the word *at* in the same way. He may say the words, print them, and point them out for you to say. Practice in many ways. Point out *an* and *at* alternately and see if Johnny reads them correctly.

Try *ap*, too. No, that's not a word, you may tell Johnny. But it says *ap* anyway.

In this lesson or in future lessons, move on to three-letter words. Teach Johnny to blend sounds together to make words such as nap, pan, tan, Nat, Nan, tat. He should practice in these ways: read words when you point, point for you to read, write words, read words he writes, and read words you write.

One day add another letter. It can be a vowel or consonant. For instance, add *o* to make several new words: not, pot, top, tot, pop.

As your chart grows, keep vowels on top and consonants on the bottom. When you need other spellings of a sound, add them below the first spelling. For instance, if you need *ck* for the name Jack, add that below a *k*. After a few weeks your chart may look like this.

a   o   i

m   n   p   t   s   j   k

nn   ck

Blending skill is one of those things you cannot hurry in children. You can't sternly shake your finger at Johnny or promise him cake if he gets it right. All you can do is give him opportunities to learn it, and one day you will see he is beginning to catch on. That's a great day. The major hurdle to reading is about to be crossed. Nurture his beginning skill. Help it grow.

During this time, use other opportunities, also, to teach the blending skill. For instance, while reading stories to Johnny, find a word or two that he can sound out himself. Stories like *The Cat in the Hat* are gold mines for this stage of reading.

If the blending skill is slow in coming, your best approach is to spend more time on "real stuff" for a while and less time on reading instruction. Later, when your child seems ready, you can return to the blending lessons. Remember the "science" children in the research study? They turned out to be better readers in the end.

Activities for Step 3

1. Basic activities are for the child to: 1) say a word or syllable when you point it out on the chart, 2) say and write what you point out, 3)

point out a word or syllable for you to read. (The chart is the row of vowels and the row of consonants which is described above.)

2. How many pronounceable ways can the child arrange a particular group of sounds you point out to her? For instance, *a, p,* and *t* can be arranged as *pat, tap,* and *apt.*

3. Point out words on the chart and have the child write each, in turn, on paper. Then copy each of her words neatly onto a card. Play one or more of these games with the cards. 1) As she reads each card to you she gets to jump one step up the stairs. As she reads through the pile a second time, she jumps back down. 2) Scramble the words on the floor or table. Read them one at a time and have the child find each word you read and hand it to you. 3) Spread out the cards, face up. Point out one of the words, sound by sound, on the chart. Have the child find and give you the word card which matches. Continue until you have all the cards. 4) Switch places. Let the child be "teacher" and point out words for you to give her.

4. Print one vowel on each of five cards of one color. (Or fewer cards if your pupil does not know all the short sounds yet.) Use another color to make several consonant cards. Turn the cards face down, mix them up, and spread them out. Let the child draw three cards and see if she can make a word. She scores a point or wins an M&M or raisin if she does. Mix the cards again and take another turn. She should eventually learn to draw one vowel card and two consonant cards and try to make a word with the vowel in the middle. Some few words may take another pattern.

5. A more elaborate version of the above game is to cover dice or blocks with tape and print letters on the tape. Make one block for vowels, using *a* twice, and make two blocks for consonants. On each consonant block, print *p, t, m, n, b,* and *f.* Roll the dice and form a word before a timer runs out or before you count to twenty. After this game becomes easy for your child, change one of the consonant blocks to include other sounds, such as *r, d, j, h, w,* and *l.*

STEP 4: Decoding

If you have taught Johnny or Jenny how to blend sounds into words, give yourself a big reward. You earned it. And don't worry about the rest of the reading steps. It's all downhill from here.

Downhill but guidance is needed.

In Step 4, you at last do the things that many people think of as the beginning of reading. You teach all the letters and their sounds. You teach letter combinations such as *ck* and *th*. If Jenny hasn't already picked up the letter names and alphabetical order, you may teach those now, too.

Why were these matters delayed until Step 4? For two important reasons. First, it is mentally stimulating for Jenny. She has a place in her mind now to put this new information. Letters and sounds are not in a dull memorized list that she can't use. But she adds them to the growing reading plan, or scheme, in her head. Second, it is efficient. When she learns a new sound now, she puts it immediately to work and reinforces her new learning. Thus she learns more easily and quickly than she would have before.

The term "optimum learning time" applies to this procedure of teaching the letters and sounds after a child knows how to use them. When you wait for the optimum time, things go easier, faster, and better.

Now if your Jenny has caught on to the idea of blending sounds together, she is ready for Step 4. There is a lot to do in Step 4. But don't panic; it's easier than Step 3.

Before we describe the things to accomplish in this step, let's review some important teaching principles.

1. Teach each new item several times and in a variety of ways. Do not expect a child to learn something just because you told her once. She will occasionally, but don't depend on it for the long list of sounds you must now teach.

2. Proceed only as fast as the child can comfortably learn. Do not overload and discourage her.

3. Use both "look and say" and "write and say" methods with

VOWEL CHART

Vowels

    a = cat, tame, want
    e = pet, me (This vowel can change other vowel sounds:
             hat to hate, bit to bite.)
    i = sit, hi
    o = on, no, do
    u = sun, cute, put
    w = sometimes acts in a vowel pair: saw, few
    y = funny, try

Vowels with *r*

er, ir, or, ur = /er/ as in her, sir, work, hurt
ar = car
or = for

Vowel pairs

ai, ay = rain, may (*y* at end of a word or syllable)
au, aw = fault, saw
ea = eat, bread, break
ee = see
ei, ey = weigh, they; ceiling, key (*y* at end of words)
eu, ew = feud, few (*w* at end of words)
ie = piece, pie
oa, oe = boat, hoe (first vowel sounds, long)
oi, oy = boil, boy (slides from one sound to the next)
oo = too, took
ou, ow = loud, cow (slides)
ue, ui = blue, suit (after *g* the *i* is sounded: guitar, guide)

CONSONANT CHART

Consonants with one sound

b	=	bat
f	=	fan
h	=	hat
j	=	jam
k	=	kit
l	=	lad
m	=	man
n	=	nap
p	=	pan
r	=	ran
t	=	tan
v	=	van
w	=	win
y	=	yes
z	=	zoo

Consonants with more than one sound

c	=	cat, cent,
d	=	dog, liked /t/, education /j/
g	=	get, gem /j/
s	=	sat, has /z/, sure /sh/
x	=	box /ks/, exact /gs/, anxiety /z/
qu	=	quack, plaque

Consonant pairs (new sounds)

ch	=	chip, chorus, chevron
gh	=	enough (at end of words)
ng	=	bang
ph	=	phone
sh	=	ship
th	=	this, thin
wh	=	why

Consonant pairs (one letter silent)

ck	=	back
gh	=	ghost (at beginning of words)
gn	=	gnaw
kn	=	know
mb	=	lamb
rh	=	rhyme
wr	=	write

(In other consonant pairs, such as *st, br,* and *ld,* both consonants have their regular sounds.)

the phonics. Be sure your child writes every day. First, words; later, sentences.

4. Make sure your child experiences success in every lesson. If you've been working on something that's too hard, then turn to an easier task before stopping work for the day.

5. Review often.

Step 4 is phonics teaching, or decoding, as teachers often say nowadays. Many people are scared of phonics. So much has been written and spoken and researched by "experts," that parents have been intimidated.

Don't you be intimidated. Realize, first of all, that phonics is not "neat." The reason you feel you have never quite mastered phonics is that nobody's system completely wraps up the loose ends for you. Each system has a different way of weaving strands together, and each has different kinds of ends left loose. So it's only natural to feel that you can't answer all the questions that may come up while you're teaching.

But you read, don't you? Somehow, by yourself or with help, you picked up enough phonics knowledge to be able to read. Phonics is no mystery. You use it every day.

Adopt a commonsense attitude that you can teach phonics as well as the next person. It doesn't matter a great deal in what order you teach the items. Far more important is a warm relationship with your pupil and a happy atmosphere surrounding reading. If you want to buy flashcards and workbooks and charts, fine. Anything on the market will help if you and your child enjoy working with the materials. Ignore the arguments about which system is best, because you're going to use an individualized system with your child. You're going to proceed at her pace. You're going to answer her questions, which may mean teaching some matters "out of order" according to a phonics system. So buy whatever you want or whatever is at hand. Or don't buy phonics materials at all. Use the money, instead, for good books.

The consonant and vowel charts will help you plan. Start with single-letter spellings. Add the others at whatever pace your child can learn them. You can teach a sound by simple homespun means. Use paper and crayon or pencil. Use a slate if you have one. Homemade flashcards work just as well as commercial ones. Show and say a sound, have Jenny say and write it. Read and write words which contain the sound. Review on the following days. That's all there is to it.

The two charts contain only seven lists, an entirely manageable number. If you wanted lists of every oddity of spelling you might encounter, the charts could be much longer, of course. But the great secret of phonics, which few dare to speak about, is that the child doesn't have to learn it all. That's right, and it's not heresy; it's only common sense. The time comes when it is more convenient for the child simply to learn the words than to learn obscure phonics rules.

For instance, you could teach the six sounds of *ough,* and when your pupil comes to the word *thought* she can try to decide which of the six sounds to say. But how cumbersome! It is much simpler just to learn the word *thought,* and to learn other "rough and tough" words: though, through, cough, bough, and enough. This is the same as learning phonics, because from each word the child can figure out others. For instance, from the word *thought* she can figure out *bought, brought,* and *fought.* In fact, in this case it works better than starting with *ough.* She is, in effect, starting with *ought,* and that has only one pronunciation and not six.

As you teach, you will bump into the messiness of phonics many times over. Say that Jenny needs help with the word *might.* Do you tell her that it's the second sound of *i,* /eye/, and a silent *gh*? Or do you tell her that *igh* says /eye/? Well, it doesn't matter which you tell her, because if she can read *might* she can figure out *fight, sight, bright, sigh,* and so forth.

Here is another messiness. What do you do with words like *motion, gracious,* and *passion*? You could teach a rule that *t, c,* and *s,* when followed by *i,* have a /sh/ sound. That's partly true. Sometimes *si* has a /zh/ sound, as in *vision.* On the other hand, you could just let Jenny learn the whole second syllable in the words mentioned. That will help her figure out numerous words that end similarly.

As a general principle, then, when you bump into a messy phonics problem, you can just teach the syllable or word at hand. That will be useful for your child, in many cases more useful than if you teach some obscure phonics rule that covers the situation.

This in essence, is the great unadvertised secret of phonics. You don't have to continue until every last phonics rule and obscure sound is mastered. You can start off systematically teaching a list of sounds. But at some point your child will take off and fly with her reading skills. She forms her own rules and doesn't need the rest that you planned to teach. Let her fly.

Sight Words

Some words of high use are not phonetically regular. It saves time to let the child simply learn these as sight words instead of trying to learn all the phonics they require. These words, in alphabetical order, are:

any	one	some
come	other	the
could	people	there
from	said	two
many	says	was
of	should	would

By grouping the sight words, you can simplify the learning task for your child. One group is:

> could
> should
> would

In another group, *o* has the sound of /uh/. If you wish, you can teach that as a fourth sound of *o*. *One* (and *once*) could be added to the group. In these two words *o* has the sound of /wuh/. This group is:

> come   one
> from
> of
> other
> some

In a third group *a,* as well as *ai* and *ay,* has the sound /eh/. This group is:

> any
> many
> said
> says

This leaves only five words to learn separately. They are:

> people
> the
> there
> two
> was

Early in Step 4, you can test your child on the above words by having her read from the list any that she knows. Make flashcards for the rest of the words—those she doesn't know—and practice them daily. Have her practice writing the words, also. If writing is a struggle for her, use short phrases such as "one ball," "two balls," "the cat," "any cat." Later, when writing becomes easier, she should write full sentences and even paragraphs.

Writing

Writing skill and reading skill grow together. Writing, in fact, is a powerful method to use in your teaching. To write, Jenny must totally concentrate. Eye, hand, and brain are used. Mental hearing and speech are involved. And if you dictate or she reads what is to be written, then actual hearing and speech are involved. Even a few minutes of writing each day will greatly enhance the learning of reading.

How do you teach writing? At earlier steps you probably wrote (printed) Jenny's name and let her trace it. This is a good way to start. Next, instead of tracing, she can copy. Later, when an image is formed in her head, she can copy from this mental image. That is, she will be able to write some words without looking at a model.

Now in Step 4, use all these teaching methods: 1) write models for the child to copy, 2) dictate models for the child to write, and 3) let the child make up her own writings. Each method is explained more fully in the following sections.

1) Copying. Print one or more full sentences for the child to copy. Be careful to use capital and small letters accurately. Teach about capitals at the beginning of sentences and periods or other marks at the end. Sources for sentences are many. You or the child can make them up or you can find them in books, poems, or songs. Try "I'll huff and I'll puff and I'll blow your house in," or "You can't catch me. I'm the gingerbread man." Use the copying method daily at first. When your child becomes proficient at copying, use the method of dictating more and more often.

2) Dictating. Dictate sentences for the child to write. From your voice inflections she must decide how to punctuate. Also she must decide about capitalizations and spellings. After she writes, give her immediate feedback by letting her see the original that you dictated from. Learn from each error. Fold back her first try and let her try again if she thinks she can do better. After she becomes proficient at writing sentences from dictation, move on to paragraphs and longer selections. Dictating from good books definitely does NOT stifle creativity. It gives your child more tools and more skill with which to be creative. Use this method regularly—at least twice a week.

3) Writing. Some children need no urging to write a story of their own, and others need much help and encouragement. So you can use more of method 3 (writing) or more of method 2 (dictating) according to the preferences of your particular pupil. Most teachers are agreed that learning proceeds better if you are not overly critical of the child's efforts at this early time in her writing career. The problems of sentence construction, spelling, punctuation, and so forth are too much to master all at once. Let the child write freely. Tell her how to spell any word she asks for. Let her spell others phonetically, even though wrong. Afterward, enjoy her story. Commend her. And make your private notes about what to teach in a future phonics or spelling lesson or other lesson.

Spelling

To teach writing you naturally need to include spelling. For the most efficient home teaching, spelling should be integrated with reading, phonics, and writing lessons. Studying lists from a spelling book is less efficient.

There are two approaches you can take to spelling. One is the phonics approach. As you teach a new sound, write, read, and spell some words which use that sound. For instance, when you are teaching the first sound of *x*, list some words that end with that sound: fox, box, fix, mix, ax, and so forth. If your pupil can handle harder words, try ones like axle, extra, and excuse. Spelling tests on "families" like this are fun and not too difficult. After a few families have been studied, have a test on words from several families. This shows if one of them might need some reviewing.

Here are some additional spelling helps which do not appear in the phonics charts. You may use these, also, for teaching spelling by the phonics approach.

1. In a syllable or word with consonant-vowel-consonant pattern, the vowel is usually short. Examples: cat, win.

2. When a single vowel ends a syllable or word, it is usually long. Examples: go, he.

NOTE: Both 1 and 2 often help you decide whether a consonant is double or not. For example: lit-tle, bri-dle. In the word *little*, the short vowel sound indicates that two *t*'s are needed, one to enclose the vowel in the first syllable and one to start the next syllable. The long vowel sound in *bridle* tells you that it should not be enclosed with an extra *d*.

3. *I* before *e* except after *c* or when sounded like /ay/ as in neighbor or weigh.

4. Change *y* to *i* before adding an ending (when the *y* is preceded by a consonant). Examples: babies, funniest, but monkeying.

5. Drop silent *e* and add *ing* or other endings which begin with a vowel.

6. When a final consonant is preceded by one vowel, double

the consonant before adding *ing* or other endings which begin with a vowel. This works with one-syllable words and with words accented on the last syllable. Examples: running, runner; beginning, but deepening.

7. On longer words, spell one syllable at a time, using whatever phonics guidelines help in each syllable.

A powerful method for teaching is to help the child figure out rules by herself. For instance, to help Jenny learn the silent *e* rule which is on the vowel chart, begin with a list of words with short vowels sounds, as in the first column below.

hat	hate
can	cane
hop	hope
bit	bite
cut	cute

Lead her to see that each word has a short vowel sound, as she probably learned previously. Then tell her to copy one of the words, add a silent *e* to it, and read her new word. Continue with more of the words, as in the second column above. Then see if she can make up a rule to explain what silent *e* does to words.

Practically everything you teach in phonics or spelling can be approached in this way, with the child figuring out things for herself. Advantages of this method are: 1) you can see whether the child understands and is not just repeating by rote, 2) the child learns thinking skills that help with future problems as well as the one at hand, 3) it results in faster learning for the child and less reteaching for you.

A second approach to spelling is called the "common word" approach. Spelling texts using this system have weekly lists of words selected from larger lists, such as "The 1000 Most Commonly Used Words." This is a convenient way to teach a classroom full of children. But there's a more efficient way to do it at home. You and your child can collect weekly lists of words from your child's own daily writing. This individualized system saves her the time of studying and being tested on words someone else in a class needs but she already knows. And it will naturally include any words in "The 1000 Most Commonly Used Words" that she can't spell yet. If a word is common, she will be using it. If she doesn't use it, it's not very common.

For a strong spelling program, use both the phonics approach and the common word approach. Mix them in any arrangement. This week have a list of words in a phonics "family." Next week use a list collected from your child's writings. Or after you collect a number of words, arrange some of them into phonics families for easier learning.

Teach handwriting along with spelling. After your child has good control of a pencil, use lined paper and insist upon correct forms for all letters. Let her continue manuscript writing (printing) for a couple of years, or until she writes quite easily and rapidly. Then you may let her switch to cursive writing. Only a few weeks are needed for the change if you wait for the optimum time.

Step 4 may last for many months or even two or three years. For some few children, most decoding skills can be mastered in a few weeks. Step 4 involves more work on your part than the next step. You must teach phonics more or less systematically. You must see that the child reads and writes every school day. It is important, also, to enjoy books with your child. Continue reading to her. Laugh together over funny books. Wonder together at the marvelous things you find in books. Gradually your child will arrive at Step 5.

Activities for Step 4

1. Activities 1, 2, and 3 given for Step 3 may each be extended now to include more sounds.

2. Start a notebook. Add pages gradually, as new sounds and phonics rules are studied. Either make one page for each consonant and vowel, and later for the pairs. Or make pages with clusters of sounds, and rules governing them. For instance, a page could list the consonants that have only one sound and another page list the consonants with more than one sound. A later page could have all the vowel pairs that begin with *a*. Refer to the pages for review. Add examples and rules whenever new information is learned.

3. When the child is learning a new sound-spelling, such as *ar,* you and she can collect a list of spelling words using the sound. (Car, start, mark, dart, alarm, farm, march.) Test her on the list. After several such lists are collected, give a test using selected words from all the lists. Review as needed.

4. Develop a dictionary or a file of spelling bears—words which are difficult to remember because they are not phonetically regular. Add to the dictionary whenever you stumble across such a word in the day's reading or writing lesson. Periodically study a group of these and

take a test on them. Don't let the list become unmanageably long. If it threatens to, weed out words that seem less useful than others.

5. Print a phonics family of words in a row or other formation and let the child read them to "swim across the river," "walk the tightrope," "go up the elevator," or "ride the roller coaster." Example, the *ng* family: sing, bang, hang, ring, hung, ping, pong, lung, rang, sang. For a more active version of this activity, print the words on cards and let the child jump up the stairsteps or walk along a balance beam as he reads each word.

6. Play a more difficult version of game 4 in the Step 3 section. Draw three consonant cards and one vowel card. If the child can make a word with all four cards she wins four M&M's. If she uses only two or three cards she wins 2 or 3 M&M's. Four-letter words will usually be in the pattern of *fast* or of *stop*. That is, the vowel appears in second or third position and two consonants blend together either before or after the vowel.

STEP 5: Fluency

Let this step overlap the previous one, as all the steps do. When your child knows the consonant sounds and the common vowel sounds and is beginning to learn about the pairs, start providing him with as much easy reading material as you can find. Let him read, read, read.

Don't be a pushy parent who forces a child into harder books than he wants. Easy books give Johnny opportunity to consolidate his knowledge and skill in the decoding matters. Easy books also help him learn and overlearn the common words in our language that are used repeatedly. These common words make up a large percentage of the vocabulary even in difficult books. But let Johnny practice them in easy books. Easy books help him gain skills in smooth and rapid reading They stimulate his thinking and his imagination. He also learns that books are fun. When he is not struggling with difficult vocabulary, he can occupy his mind with the content of stories and books. And even at this easy level, wide vistas of information, ideas, and attitudes begin to open up for him.

But remember, gaining information from books is not the main purpose during this step. That comes later. The main purpose now is to read, read, read, so that decoding skills become overlearned and automatic.

What about comprehension? If you have followed any debates on reading instruction, you probably have heard that you should be teaching something called "comprehension." Some people even say that you shouldn't teach so much phonics; you should be teaching comprehension, instead. But don't worry about that. If your child laughs at something in a book, he is comprehending it. If he asks a question, he is thinking and comprehending. If he sometimes chooses his own books, on dinosaurs or whatever, he is comprehending. The point the "comprehension" people miss is that the child uses easy books during his early steps in reading. Of course he comprehends them.

The truth in this debate, as you have no doubt seen, is that phonics has its place in the early stages of reading, and comprehension can be emphasized later. Just now, in Step 5, your child should gain fluency. This is a step that many people try to skip. They keep pushing on to the hard stuff.

As was mentioned earlier, you may let this step overlap with Step 4. So that means you are still carrying on systematic phonics lessons. Teach the consonant and vowel pairs one at a time. Also teach any other phonics that your child bumps into in his reading. This individualized teaching may not seem very systematic, but it is highly efficient. When Johnny meets a problem and you help him solve it, that is a strong learning episode. The item will require less reteaching and less review. So that is a "system" of teaching phonics. It is a powerful method, individualized, and especially suited for home teaching.

Here is a list of basic activities your child can do during this step. Using all of them from time to time will give variety to your lessons.

> Spell words from dictation.
> Copy sentences from your model.
> Write sentences from dictation.
> Find a particular word or sentence that you read from a page.
> From a page, find the answer to a question that you ask.
> Read aloud with good expression.
> Read silently, tell about the story, then read aloud.
> Write an original story.
> Draw a picture to illustrate the original story.
> Learn a new phonics rule when an unusual word is encountered.
> Listen to you read stories.

Also, for variety from time to time, you can use game and activity ideas in Step 4, as well as the new activities given at the end of this Step 5 section.

Evaluating Your Child's Reading

When you work with your child daily, you should feel little need to test him. You know how well he reads orally. You know what decoding skills you have tried to teach but he still forgets. You know if he is plunging on ahead, not seeming to need any more phonics. The truth is, you know more about his reading than most tests will tell you.

But one question still lurks in the back of many parents' minds. They want to know how Johnny compares with other children his age. Comparisons are a bit tricky, because there is wide variation in the abilities of children of any particular age or grade. And they are really not as helpful as other concepts about reading levels. But this evaluation section will suggest some simple, informal ways to compare your child's reading with average grade levels. It also will suggest a second concept of reading levels which you will use practically every teaching day.

The second concept is to understand that your child has three reading levels at all times. These have been called his 1) independent level, 2) instructional level, and 3) frustration level. This is more a way to rate books than to rate Johnny. The books Johnny can read by himself are on his independent level. The books you might use to teach him new skills are on his instructional level. And the books too hard even for that are at his frustration level.

Like Goldilocks, you might say, "This book is to-o-o hard. This book is to-o-o easy. But this book is ju-u-st right." You can teach Johnny to identify books too hard for him. But the other levels are only for your planning, not for his. No child ever says, "This book is to-o-o easy," all on his own. If spoken at all, it is from a child of pushy parents, a child who has heard remarks about him reading baby books. This is not a natural reaction to books. We adults don't pick up a "Reader's Digest" and say, "This is to-o-o easy." The fact is, we probably pick it up at the end of a busy day because we want some easy, relaxing reading. Let Johnny have that same privilege of reading for enjoyment. In this fluency step of reading, you want him to read lots of easy books.

To determine whether a book is too hard, count off a section of 100 words and ask the child to read it to you. If he is unable to read more than five of the words, the book is on his frustration level. He can be taught a form of this test, himself, as a useful means of selecting library books. He simply reads a page and counts on his fingers the words he does not know. If he runs out of fingers on one hand, including his thumb, the book is likely to be harder than he wants. This system assumes that the page will have from 100 to 200 words on it.

If the child misses from three to five words on your 100 word sample, you may consider the book to be on his instructional level. It is just right. Never assume that the harder a book is, the more a child can learn from it. A book that stretches and challenges, but does not frustrate, is the best choice for teaching.

You can test further, by asking questions about the sample selection. Keeping score on questions is more complicated, but you can learn to estimate. If the word count indicates you have a book on the instructional level, try asking a few questions. If the child answers about three out of four, this confirms the diagnosis. It shows he understands a lot of what he reads, but there is still room for you to teach something.

For your quick reference, a chart of this testing procedure follows.

	Words Missed	Questions Missed
Independent reading level:	0 to 2%	up to 10%
Instructional reading level:	3 to 5%	up to 25%
Frustration reading level:	over 5%	over 25%

It may take a little time to clearly understand what those levels are all about. But try scoring some library books or even some of your child's textbooks and see what the scores tell you. If textbooks are at his frustration level, this will explain the trouble he's been having.

After you have in your head a good picture of the above levels, move on to this next concept, called the "expectancy level." This is a highly significant concept understood by relatively few people. It tells whether your child is doing as well as you should expect him to.

Wouldn't you give a lot for that information? If you knew your child should be doing better, you would start looking for the problem. Does he need more phonics? Does he need a better attitude and more time spent on reading? Does he need the help of a skilled opthamologist or other professional? You would find the trouble, remedy it, and bring the child up to his expectancy level. On the other hand, if you find he is reading up to expectancy level already, you can relax. If you've been pushing, you can slow down and allow him more time to grow into advanced reading levels.

To find the expectancy level, you can use the same 100 word samples you counted off for the child to read. Or similar samples will do. But this time you read aloud to the child. Then ask him about the meaning of words in the selection. Also ask other questions. And score exactly as in the chart above. You now know whether the child has vocabulary enough and understanding enough to read a particular book. If the score shows that you should "expect" him to read the book, but he can't, then you have a teaching problem to solve. If the score shows that he doesn't understand the book even when you read it to him, then don't expect him to read it . . . yet.

With the concept of expectancy, you sometimes can get useful information from an achievement test the child takes at school. Some of these tests, in the subheadings under "reading," have a score for a test in which the teacher read the words. Ask about each subhead, and if you find one like this, treat it as an expectancy score. For example, if your child scored fourth grade level in that subtest but only third grade level in reading overall, you may suspect that he needs more phonics or something to bring his reading up to the expectancy level.

Now we turn to the tricky concept of comparing your child's reading with grade levels. One simple way to do this is to use the same procedure as above, but do the testing from a series of graded reading textbooks. Borrow the books from your local school or from the public library. If your child is third grade age, for instance, you should get readers from first grade, second grade, and so on up for as high as you think he may be able to read. Use 100 word samples from the middle of each book and test as described above to find which book meets his instructional level.

This gives you a rough idea of how far the child has progressed. But the tricky part is that it doesn't tell you what grade he should be in. That's because in any fourth grade, for instance, some children will read at first or second grade level and others may read at eighth grade level or even higher. What is called "fourth grade level" really is just a point at the middle of the class. So if your child is fourth grade age but scores about third grade on reading tests, that doesn't mean he flunked fourth grade. It just means he is below the middle. Everybody can't be above the middle. Only half the class can be there.

If your fourth grader scores sixth grade level, it doesn't mean he should be promoted to sixth grade where he would be at the middle. Let him stay in fourth and be above the middle. If you are teaching him at home, you should get more challenging books, though, in subjects requiring reading. That, of course, is an advantage of tutoring individually at home. You can more easily adapt the teaching to fit the child.

It is best not to concern yourself much with testing until at least third grade. In the first two grades children can score quite differently on tests depending on whether they are learning by a phonics method or by a sight word method. Also, in the first two grades children often need pauses for consolidation of their learning. They may pause and spurt at different times. During summer vacation after first grade, children forget a lot that must be reviewed and relearned the next year. And children are not all ready to begin reading at the same age. All these variables make it unwise to test young children and compare them with other children or with a grade level. When states or local school districts require testing of home schooled children, they often are flexible with young children and will postpone testing if you request it.

If you have gone through the five steps in this guide, if your child can blend sounds together, has learned quite a lot of phonics, and has spent time gaining fluency, then you might wish to test or have some professional testing done. If you do, use the test results wisely. They are not a club to beat your child with. They are not to brag to friends about. The only sensible use is to gain information that might be helpful in planning future lessons for the child.

Activities for Step 5

1. Plan regular trips to the library with your child and treat these occasions as high-level family outings. You can go off to choose books for yourself while the child attends a story hour or plays with puppets or chooses his books. Take home some easy books he will read himself, one or two harder ones you will read to him, and perhaps a science book which he cannot read but which has beautiful pictures to learn from. On the way home stop for ice cream or pizza or whatever rates high in your family. Back home again, the next reading lesson is "free reading," in which the child is allowed time to simply read for fun from his new library selections. It's all right if he rejects a book once he starts reading it. We adults do that all the time.

2. Now and then, when your budget can stand it, take a family excursion to a bookstore. Let your child grow up learning that families buy books as well as records and sports equipment and other recreational items.

3. Prepare your child to get the most out of a book. This means, whenever possible, you will read it first. (You can learn to skim rapidly through most children's books, so this is not an impossible addition to your schedule.) If the book is set in another country or in the long ago or is about an unfamiliar subject, tell him a little about these matters. Introduce him to new words and ideas he will encounter in the book, not so much preteaching that you spoil the book for him, but just enough to strengthen and direct his interest.

4. While you are reading a book to the child, occasionally ask what he thinks will happen next. Why? Discuss the characters. Does the child like each person? Why or why not? Does he like the way the story ends? When you read the same stories your child does, you will find opportunities to talk about values that are important in the life of your family. This, perhaps, is the main reason you are teaching the child at home. Be careful, though, not to belabor these matters. Use a light touch, and only some of the books.

5. On family trips, arrange time to stop at factories, mines, or other businesses and ask about tours. Even those which don't have regular tours are often happy to show off for interested people. Museums, botanical gardens, and other public places are also good for extending

your child's learning, especially when taken in small bites. All new experiences extend your child's vocabulary and knowledge and make him a better reader. On trips, also, don't pass up the many opportunities to learn map reading.

6. Don't wait for vacations, but plan mini-trips close to home. Will a friend in the bank take your child to see a vault? Is there a slough nearby where water backs up from a river? And for extending vocabulary, what about the baking powder, garlic buds, furnace filters, or carburetor around your house and garage? Have you dried dandelion roots and crushed them for tea? Opportunity for learning new words is endless. In fact, you can hardly stop your child from learning them. Just don't keep him bent over spelling papers, vocabulary workbooks, and difficult books. Let him freely learn from real life.

7. The child may read aloud to a younger sibling or friend. If you can pull this off, he will be reviewing the fun and phonics of nursery rhymes and other "babyish" literature that he might not read otherwise.

8. Sometimes when your child makes up stories of his own, especially when he has a long story, write it for him. Let him dictate while you get it down. Use a typewriter or word processor if you have one. Later, share the stories with someone. Have them read at the family dinner table; mail some to Grandma or a friend. Authors need an audience.

9. Make occasions for letter writing. Have the child write to a relative, send for free samples or for mail order items, write to a newspaper or the mayor about a current controversy, write to a TV station to give opinions about their programing.

10. Help the child make a book about one of his hobbies. Each page, for instance, might describe one of the rocks in his collection and remind him about where and how he found it.

A Final Word

Finally, congratulations are due to you for taking your child up the steps from prereading through decoding and fluency. Your greater reward is that your child has as fine a start in reading as he could get anywhere. He now has learned to read. From this point on, he can read to learn. A path toward a richer, more meaningful life for him now leads into the years ahead.